# WHISKEY TANGO FOXTROT

By Rebecca Crookshank

Supported using public funding by
**ARTS COUNCIL ENGLAND**

**STAGE ONE**

**ROYAL AIR FORCE theatrical association**

CROWDSHED

**Whiskey Tango Foxtrot** premiered at the Underbelly Cowgate, Edinburgh Fringe Festival 2015, followed by a UK tour in 2016 to the following venues:

Anselm Studios, *Canterbury*
Fisher Theatre, *Bungay*
Attenborough Centre, *Leicester*
Drill Hall, *Lincoln*
Derby Theatre, *Derby*
Ashcroft Arts Centre, *Fareham*
Old Fire Station, *Oxford*
Back Door @ The Secombe, *Sutton*
Rose and Crown, *London*
Tristan Bates, *London*
Cast, *Doncaster*
Barbican Theatre, *Plymouth*
Brewhouse, *Taunton*
Dukebox Theatre, *Brighton*

With special thanks to Arts Council England, Stage One, Royal British Legion Women's Section, Royal Air Force Theatrical Association (RAFTA), British Forces Broadcasting Services (BFBS), Forces TV and CrowdShed who all supported the development and premiere of *Whiskey Tango Foxtrot*.

## Cast:
All roles played by Rebecca Crookshank

## Creative Team:

| | |
|---|---|
| Writer | Rebecca Crookshank |
| Producer | Oliver Taheri Productions |
| Director/Dramaturg | Jessica Beck |
| Assistant Director | Katharina Reinthaller |
| Designer | Alberta Jones / Cherry Truluck |
| Dress Design | Anne Sophie Cochevelou |
| Lighting/Sound | Phil Hewitt |
| Photography | Cecilia Cooper-Colby |
| Artwork | Fin Irwin |
| PR | Chloe Nelkin Consulting |

## Rebecca Crookshank: Writer/Performer

Rebecca is an artist based in East London. Alongside her writing and performing, she runs her own creative consultancy company encouraging equality, the arts and future voices. Clients include the Royal Ballet, The International School of Harrow Beijing, Jacksons Lane, LAMDA and Arts Award. She also works as a writer in residence at Frederick Bremer School. *Whiskey Tango Foxtrot* marks her debut play as a solo writer/performer and was nominated for Best New Play, Best New Production, Best Director and Best Actress in the 2015 Broadway World Awards. Her first short play *Clipping My Wings* premiered at the 'Our Bodies Our Future' Conference in 2015 led by MP Stella Creasy.

Theatre credits include: Claire in *Etiquette & Vitriol* (Soho Theatre, London); Dick Whittington in *Poppy* (Landor Theatre, London); Rhianna in *England Street* by Kenny Emson; Lindsey in *LBW* directed by Fin Irwin; *Tin Girls* directed by Jessica Beck (all for The Bike Shed Theatre); Dorcas & Brigitta in *Loveplay* (Rose & Crown); Bianca in *Taming of The Shrew* (St Leonard's Church–Shoreditch) both for New Rep Company; Kelly in *Impotent* (Lion & Unicorn) and Lady Bracknell in *The Importance of Being Ernest* (St James Theatre).

As Writer: *Whiskey Tango Foxtrot* (Underbelly, Edinburgh and UK tour); *Alice: A New Musical* (St James Theatre); *Crookshank and Finlay comedy sketch show* (in development).

Film, Radio & TV credits include: Tim Burton's *Alice in Wonderland* (Universal); *Casualty* (BBC) directed by Nigel Douglas and Robson Green's *Extreme Fishing* (Channel 5).

For more information about her work please visit: rebeccacrookshank.com and follow @RJCrookshank, @WTFtheplay & @Rebeccaconsults

## Oliver Taheri Productions: Producer

OTP was founded in 2013 by entrepreneur and commercial theatre producer Oliver Taheri.

In 2013 OTP produced the critically acclaimed sell out world premiere of *Impotent* (Lion and Unicorn) ahead of the multi-award-nominated *Spring Tide* (Old Red Lion) later that year. Other productions include the first London revival of David Hare's *The Vertical Hour* (Park Theatre–Time Out Critics' Choice) starring Peter Davison and directed by BAFTA winner Nigel Douglas; *Alice: A New Musical* (St James Theatre); European Premiere of Tony Award-winning musical *Urinetown* directed by Jamie Lloyd (St James & Apollo West End); Jonathan Harvey's *Beautiful Thing* (UK Tour) and critically acclaimed *Whiskey Tango Foxtrot* (Underbelly, Edinburgh-4 Broadway World Award Nominations).

2016 saw the launch of OTP Films, with the first project *The Library* being entered into international film festivals. The second project, feature film *Julie and Jane*, is due to shoot in late 2016.

OTP is committed to providing high quality theatre and film productions for UK and global audiences and is dedicated to the producing and staging of ambitious, thought provoking productions.

For more info, visit olivertaheriproductions.com

## Jessica Beck: Director/Dramaturg

Jessica Beck is an American-born theatre artist, living and working in the UK for over a decade as a freelance director and somatic practitioner. Specialising in new writing and devised work, Jessica is an Artistic Associate of The Bike Shed Theatre, Exeter, and formally an Associate of Theatre503 (2004-2010).

Directing and dramaturgy credits include: *Whiskey Tango Foxtrot* – Broadway World UK/West End Award Nominations: Best New Play, New Production, Director, and Leading Actress (Edinburgh Festival/UK Tour); *Normal/Madness* by Fiona Geddes (Scottish Tour/Edinburgh Festival); *Icarus in Love* by Edson Burton, *The Exeter Blitz Project* by Jessica Beck and Helena Enright, *Tin Girls* with photographer Alice Carfare (The Bike Shed Theatre); *Alice's Adventures in the New World* by Sarah Sigal (Old Red Lion, UK Tour); *Ein Abend Mit Ruby* with the Ruby Dolls (Jermyn Street Theatre); *Up The Gary* by Andrew Barron and Jessica Beck (Theatre503/ Edinburgh/UK Tour/NYC) and *Terrorist! The Musical* (Edinburgh).

Other directing credits include: *Less Than a Year* by Helena Enright (The Bike Shed Theatre); *Play* and *Footfalls* by Samuel Beckett (University of Exeter); *2002* by Nimer Rashed and *2008* by Phil Porter for *Decade* (Theatre503); *Zoo* by Dawn King (Union Theatre); *Dogfight* by Sarah Sigal (Arcola Theatre/Edinburgh); *The Whale and the Bird* by Greta Clough, and *All Alone* by Gene David Kirk (Edinburgh/Project Arts Centre, Dublin/Soho Playhouse, NYC).

Recipient of The New York Fringe Festival Excellence Award for Outstanding Direction 2007. Jessica teaches directing, acting, and the Feldenkrais Method of Somatic Education.

For more information about her work please visit: www.facebook.com/drjessicabeck and follow @mizbeck

## Katharina Reinthaller: Assistant Director

Katharina Reinthaller is a freelance director and dramaturg based in London who trained at University of Vienna and with StoneCrabs Theatre Company (graduate of Young Directors' Programme 2013/14).

Directing work includes: *LABELS* (Edinburgh Fringe Festival, Pleasance Courtyard, Winner of The Scotsman Fringe First Award, The Holden Street Theatre Award, shortlisted for Amnesty Internationals Freedom of Speech Award); *Eat When You Can, Sleep When You Can* (Vienna/Dubai); *A Gaggle of Saints* (The Albany Studio, London) and *Fascination* (The Arcola Theatre).

She is currently the Assistant Director of *Whiskey Tango Foxtrot* (Edinburgh Fringe Festival, Underbelly, UK Tour 2016) and Associate Director of Kidder's Production *Normal/Madness* (Edinburgh Fringe 2014/Scotland Tour 2015) as well as a creative associate of Worklight Theatre.

## Alberta Jones: Designer

Alberta Jones is a theatre designer, art director, illustrator and maker. She has worked on many productions and recently completed a successful spring tour with her design for *A Strange Wild Song* created with the critically acclaimed Rhum and Clay Theatre Company.

Other production designs include: *Man in the Moone* (UK Tour) and *A Premature Feeding Led to His Consumption* (Robin Howard Theatre).

As a theatre design associate Alberta has worked on many shows alongside Cherry Truluck including *All.That Fall*, directed by Trevor Nunn (West End/New York). Other shows include: *Soldiers Wives* (Roxy Downstairs, Assembly); *Mother Adam* (Jermyn Street Theatre); *Mary Rose* (Riverside Studios); *The Taming of the Shrew* (Southwark Playhouse) and *Don Giovanni* (Soho Theatre).

To find out more about Alberta please visit: albertajones.com

## Cherry Truluck: Designer

Cherry Truluck has worked as a freelance Designer and Art Director for ten years. For the last five years, she has focused on live and theatrical brand experiences, creating events for major corporations and independent clients, whilst also building an impressive theatre design portfolio.

As a theatre designer, Cherry has recently designed Samuel Beckett's *All That Fall*, directed by Trevor Nunn and starring Eileen Atkins and Michael Gambon, which transferred to New York (59E59) in November 2013 following successful runs at Jermyn Street Theatre and The Arts Theatre, London. Other recent projects include *Martine* (Finborough Theatre); *The Notorious Mrs Ebbsmith* (Jermyn Street Theatre); *Thark* (Park Theatre) for which she was nominated Best Set Designer 2013 in the OffWestend Awards; *Religion and Anarchy* (written and co-directed by Steven Berkoff); *The Potsdam Quartet* (Jermyn Street Theatre) and a second instalment of *The Exeter Blitz Project* (The Bike Shed Theatre).

## Phil Hewitt: Lighting/Sound

Phil Hewitt has designed lighting and sound for well over 50 productions, both in the UK, and abroad. Collaborations with director Jessica Beck include: *Normal/Madness* (Edinburgh/Scottish Tour); *The Exeter Blitz Project* (The Bike Shed Theatre); *Alice's Adventures in the New World* (Old Red Lion/UK Tour); *Up the Gary* (Edinburgh/UK Tour/NYC); *Zoo* (Union Theatre); *Dogfight* (Arcola/Edinburgh); *All Alone* (Edinburgh/Dublin/NYC) and *Terrorist! The Musical* (Edinburgh).

## Writer's acknowledgements:

I would like to thank Beaford Arts in North Devon and the Breathing Space programme where this show began its life in 2009 with support and encouragement from Kate Edwards, Hannah Ashwell, David Lane and Gill and Bill from Multi Story Theatre Company. I'd also like to thank Nigel Douglas for encouraging me to work on a screenplay version and having belief in my work and voice as a writer. Rachael Bhebhe, Tony Wright and the team at the Royal British Legion Women's Section for being so generous with their time, supporting the development by providing space and linking me with their members who do fantastic work for the welfare of military families every day. The Tristan Bates First Festival and the Hen and Chickens in London for championing the scratch showings and previews. Charlotte Josephine for taking time to share her experience as a writer/performer and inspiring me to get on with making it. Arts Council England, who through supporting the development, initiated my journey as a writer/performer, enabled me to creatively unravel this personal story and continue to share it with developing audiences. Chloe, and her supersonic team at Chloe Nelkin Consultancy, and the Channel 4 news team, for their support and invitation to speak out.

**I would also like to thank the following humans;** The whole creative team – Juliet Bravo, Oscar Tango, Papa Hotel, Kilo Romeo, November Mike and Juliet Mike (Nina and James Marshall), Team Charlie November Charlie (Chloe Nelkin Consultancy), Alberta Jones, Cherry Truluck, Cecilia and Jules Cooper-Colby, Fin Irwin, Brian Astbury, Anne-Sophie Cochevelou, Joby Ingram-Dodd, Jen Malarkey, Peta Lily, Kate 'Peg' Edwards, Emma Finlay, David Lane, Joe Sellman-Leava, Marina Dixon and the fabulous Underbelly team. The late and great Joan Hopkins, Hazel Kingswood and Alysham & District branch RBLWS, Jeffrey Ayling, The Spirit of Coltishall Association, The RAF Radar Museum, RAF Museum Colindale, The tour guide on Long Island Farm East Falkland Islands, Jamie Gordon, Ali Gibson, BFBS Radio and Forces TV, Michael Brash from Pathfinder at Baltic Publications, Natalie O'Donoghue, Jello Biafra, Barry Gordon, Dean McDonald, Leander Camesasca, Leah Rhodes, David Pearson from Nederlander Theatres, The Dominion Theatre, Christine Preece, David Marshall (for inspiring the title!), Theatre Royal Stratford East, Tom Siracusa, Colin Blumenau, Julian Stoneman, Deborah Colvin and Frederick Bremer School, A Borough United steering group, Stuart Cox and all at Jacksons Lane.

All of our wonderful CrowdShed funders: Henry and Joey Freeman, Deborah and Martin Horswill, Tom and Michelle Crookshank, Eric Crookshank, John and Tracie Crookshank, Luke Taheri and Gemma Falla, Javad Taheri, Alex Taheri and Laura Preston, Vicki and Andre Gibbs, Laurence Lord, Matt Wood, Dena Chadderton, Sophia Darke (thank you for the 'dangling in the dust' reminder), Rowan Lawrence, Lindy Davis-Berry, Cynthia Lacey, Tim Culverhouse, Nick Warren, Jenny and Paul Johnson, Jim Watts, Hilary Taheri and Andy Sharpe, Joan and Eddie Watts, Anne Coulstock, Roger and Chris Watts,

Eleanor McRea, James Gurd, Dearest Constance Cullen (and your hawk eyes), Aaron Frazer, Diane Frazer, Al the dog, Desmond, Anne Hall, Don Cotter, Arthur Duncan, Phil Parker, Marie Beck, Andrew Mitchell, Stuart Slicer, Anita Parry, Peter Ellis, Simon Egerton, Carol Harrison, Sam Dunham, Steven Lucas, Martin Truss, Nigel Douglas, Toby Dickinson, Jane Hardman-Ferris, Daryl Bennett, all the clients of Rebecca Crookshank Consultancy, students and future voices from the SHAC and Shacademy, all my dearest family, friends and those who have believed in my vision to do something more creative ...

And finally to Harry, Lara, Henry and Isabelle – the next generation of first penguins.

# Reviews

### ★★★★★ Edinburgh Evening News
'You will come across plenty shows covering sexual harassment, alcohol abuse and feminism. Few of them, however, will have the talent, subtlety, and craft of Rebecca Crookshank.'

### ★★★★★ The New Current
'For those women signing up today they may add Rebecca Crookshank on their list of women who have inspired and have been unafraid to speak out about their abuse which will go to ensuring that women no longer get treated as second class service personnel.'

### ★★★★ The List
' ... the verve and gusto she brings to her story marks her out as a considerable talent to watch.'

### ★★★★ Broadway Baby
'What sets this apart is Crookshank's immense charm, snappy comic timing and her ability to bounce between distinctly drawn characters and voices.'

### ★★★★ Edinburgh Guide
'This is a true life tale engagingly told with military precision.'

### ★★★★ UK Theatre Web
'Her bravery in confronting the former and in exposing it for us as part of this show is very real, very raw, unlike most shows she is not revealing someone else's weaknesses but her own.'

### ★★★★ Theatre Fullstop
'A touching piece written and performed from the heart which keeps the audience enthralled from start to finish'

**Nominated for 4 awards:**
*Best New Play*
*Best New Production*
*Best Leading Actress*
*Best Direction*

## A note from the writer

When I began writing what was to become *Whiskey Tango Foxtrot*, I never imagined the response my story would provoke. The process of putting it all together was tougher than any assault course I have faced, but the breakthroughs far outweighed the slow combat crawls across the page and onto the stage. Facilitated by my fantastic Director/Dramaturg Jessica Beck, I would speak a lot, write too much, laugh a bit, break out into a rage, feel terror and then write some more, this I realize was necessary. The first scratch sharing in February 2015 evoked genuine terror, I was petrified and I hadn't even included the darker material about what had happened to me on Mount Alice. Once audiences began to engage with my work, offer feedback and search for more truth, I started to unravel, move closer to the core of the story and it felt right to talk about it. Talk about it all.

In January 2016 I was invited by the Channel 4 News team to talk about my experiences of bullying and sexual harassment in the armed forces. This was a great opportunity to speak out to a wider audience especially those who had been affected and share some of the video archives I had included in the show.

With over 4.5 million views online in one week, and thousands more engaging with the show, my story has provoked urgent discussions and encouraged others who have been affected by bullying and sexual harassment in institutions to speak out. Supported by Arts Council England throughout the whole development, I have been able to rediscover my story and the truth of what it is I want to say. I never visualized the power of this truth, my determination for zero tolerance and courage to creatively speak out. I wanted to create a solo show about a female experience, I thought I had a fairly interesting one, the momentum gathered, Edinburgh audiences told me their own stories and the show got other people talking. I am so grateful to the arts; the power of creativity shines into the face of adversity and for me holds more weight than an official complaint.

From the list of acknowledgements you can see that there are so many people who make a production like this possible. Thank you again to everyone and anyone I have missed. My work with young people is integral to this piece and I am privileged to learn from future voices, all of you contribute and expand the creative vision. Wingwoman, Nina, you're an inspiration to us all and our treasured friendship inspired this piece of art, I bet you didn't think that would happen when we met at the NAAFI. Jessica, thank you, I believe you now, it IS all about the process and I continue to be taken by surprise.

My dear precious family across the miles; Mum, you were right 'Something more creative' you're a dynamo and your majestic energy fuels my flight. Martin and Tracie, I salute you both for so many things but ultimately making my Mum and Dad so happy. Granddad Eric and my late Grandma Eileen, thank you for continually asking me 'are you winning,' I'll keep on trying! Dad, you really are top notch, I'm inspired by your determination and your story. Michelle and little brother Tom, thank you for creating the ultimate first penguin Henry Crookshank, my darling nephew who was born right in the middle of the Edinburgh run. Thank you all for your support, you've believed in my vision and tried to make it less painful to share and speak of things that hurt.

There are two other people of whom I owe so much; Firstly my late and treasured Nanny, Patti Wicks, she introduced me to the power of the arts, encouraged me to write, shared her wit, and tendency to fantasize.

And finally, my husband Oliver Mohsen-Taheri, you are a wonder, you listen, you feel the weight like I do, together we can jump, be 'graceful, aerodynamic, exquisite'.

Thank you.

Rebecca Crookshank
2016

SACW Bludgell post
Karaoke competition

Crooky and
penguin Joan

Crooky sends out love
over the airwaves on BFBS

The
Regiment
Corporal

Sqn. Ldr. Wilton – Scramble Scramble Scramble

Wingwoman
on JAAWSC

Rebecca at the
RAF Museum with
her penguin collection

*Per ardua ad astra* – through adversity to the stars...

Rebecca as the late Joan Hopkins in the
Anne Sophie Cochevelou dress creation

For Patti and Eileen

WHISKEY TANGO FOXTROT

# WHISKEY TANGO FOXTROT

Rebecca Crookshank

OBERON BOOKS
LONDON

WWW.OBERONBOOKS.COM

First published in 2016 by Oberon Books Ltd
521 Caledonian Road, London N7 9RH
Tel: +44 (0) 20 7607 3637 / Fax: +44 (0) 20 7607 3629
e-mail: info@oberonbooks.com
www.oberonbooks.com

A catalogue record for this book is available from the British
Library.

PB ISBN: 9781783197200
E ISBN: 9781783197217

Photography: Cecilia Cooper-Colby
Artwork: Fin Irwin

Printed and bound by 4edge Limited, UK.
eBook conversion by CPI Group (UK) Ltd, Croydon, CR0 4YY.

Visit www.oberonbooks.com to read more about all our books
and to buy them. You will also find features, author interviews and
news of any author events, and you can sign up for e-newsletters
so that you're always first to hear about our new releases.

# Characters

## CROOKSHANK

A girl. Ten days after her seventeenth birthday she joins the Royal Air Force to escape her parent's divorce, small town gossip and convention. Naïve, but determined, she marches through her personal battles, embraces her creative instincts and reaches for the stars.

## REBECCA

A woman. Years later and now a civilian, revisits her journey as a young airwoman. She awakens her creative and feminist voice, draws on the highs and lows of military life and the unacceptable behaviour in an institutionalised environment.

## WINGWOMAN

The best friend. A new recruit, just seventeen years old. Half German half scouse, drinks tea with every meal and has a serious blushing problem. Also known as 'Brigitta Bieber' or 'Biffa' by Cpl. Bunting. The nickname sticks until Crookshank calls her Wingwoman. Crookshank and Wingwoman become friends for life.

## CORPORAL. BUNTING-

The parade drill and training instructor. A fierce female from Scotland, tasked with training the new recruits. She thrives on the power of her rank and status amongst the recruits.

## REGIMENT CORPORAL

The weapons expert. Trains the new recruits to kill. Enjoys flirting and taking advantage of his position of power. He's fit and passionate about being in the field, his knowledge of firearms and protein shakes is impressive.

## SQUADRON LEADER WILTON

An exchange officer. In charge of the Aerospace System Operation's squadron. On tour from the Australian Air Force on exchange in the UK. She champions non-commissioned recruits who show potential and encourages them to fly up through the ranks. An inspirational feminist.

## SENIOR AIRCRAFT WOMAN BLUDGELL

The mentor. Also working in Aerospace System Operations and in charge of the female accommodation. Originally from Barnsley she is unmarried, single and in her thirties. She enjoys letting her hair down by entering karaoke competitions and instigating drinking games.

## JOAN HOPKINS

The Spirit Guide. The first female station commander in the Royal Air Force. She appears as a hallucination in Crookshank's head but is referenced throughout the play. She continues to inspire a generation of military personnel in Trade Group 12 and left a legacy after her death. A positive role model.

## SANDY

The tour guide. A 9th generation Falkland Islander, who runs the guided tours of the island. Windswept, leathery skin and out-doorsy. Stoically British, she keeps dog biscuits, a head torch and poop bags in her pockets and has a passion for her personal slide collection and penguins.

## MOUNT ALICE MAN

The bully. An Army signaller of low rank. Posted to a remote radar site for the whole four-month detachment. He's bored but thrilled when a new girl comes up to the mountain. He leads the pack with his bullish behaviour, a tactic for survival; he wants to be the man of the mountain.

# ROYAL AIR FORCE RANK STRUCTURE

## *NON-COMMISSIONED RANKS*
### *(From low to high)*

Aircraftman/woman (**AC/ACW**)

Leading Aircraftman/woman (**LAC/LACW**)

Senior Aircraftman/Woman/Technician (**SAC/SACW/ SAC TECH**)

Junior Technician (**Jnr Tech**)

Corporal (**Cpl**)

Sergeant (**Sgt**)

Chief Technician (**Chf Tech**)

Flight Sergeant (**FS**)

Warrant Officer (**WO**)

## *COMMISSIONED RANKS – OFFICERS*

Pilot Officer (**Plt Off**)

Flying Officer (**Fg Off**)

Flight Lieutenant (**Flt Lt**)

Squadron Leader (**Sqn Ldr**)

Wing Commander (**Wg Cdr**)

Group Captain (**Gp Capt**)

Air Commodore (**Air Cdre**)

Air Vice-Marshal (**AVM**)

Air Marshal (**Air Mshl**)

Air Chief Marshal (**Air Chf Mshl**)

Marshal of the Royal Air Force (**MRAF**)

*Key*

\* For arms drill. After each command the relevant arms drill
is performed by the actor.

The Phonetic Alphabet.          I SPELL

A - Alpha                R - ROMEO
B - BRAVO                S - SIERRA
C - CHARLIE              T - TANGO
D - DELTA                U - UNIFORM
E - ECCO                 V - VICTOR
F - FOXTROT              W - WHISKEY
G - GOLF                 X - X-RAY
H - HOTEL                Y - YANKEE
I - INDIA                Z - ZULU
J - JULIET
K - KILO
L - LIMA                 ~~ROMEO~~  CHARI
M - MIKE
N - NOVEMBER
O - OSCAR                ZERO...
P -                      S ZERO
Q - QUABEC

Rebecca's original basic training notes
detailing the NATO phonetic alphabet.
The 'P' is missing (P = PAPA).

*REBECCA/CROOKSHANK shifts throughout the play as herself (now REBECCA) and then CROOKSHANK. Narrating the story from the past and present. Dressed in green overalls, a NO.1 WRAF hat, she greets the audience as CPL BUNTING, a Royal Air Force drill and training instructor from Scotland. She directs the audience to their seats as if new recruits on their first day of training. Underscored by military music from the band of the Royal Air Force. As the audience become more settled the actor improvises until clearance is given.*

CPL BUNTING: Welcome to RAF Halton. Teach. Learn. Apply.

*CROOKSHANK takes off CPL BUNTING's hat introduces herself in the present and sets up her story.*

REBECCA: That's Corporal Bunting, you'll see more of her later. Hi, I'm Rebecca. I used to be in the Royal Air Force, a trained killer … *(She makes eyes at the audience.)* People often don't believe me so I decided to make a show about it. I'm thirty-five, I'm a woman and I like to spread my wings. My teachers at school used to say 'Rebecca has a tendency to fantasize' I left as soon as I could. Welcome to my show. Let's set the scene. *(Sounds of tornados on the runway.)* It's 1997. The death of Princess Diana. The dawn of a new era *('Things can only get better' by D:REAM is played, she grooves a bit)*, remember that? I wasn't even old enough to vote. But I was old enough to join the Royal Air Force. And this ladies and gentleman is my story.

*CROOKSHANK picks up her kit bag and arranges props. Original footage of aircraft is projected onto a large radar screen hanging stage left as an original video clip is played. 'Back in the dark days'.*

*PROJECTION CLIP: RAF HALTON. (V.O.) Back in the dark days of the early 1940s the skies over Britain droned with the sound of aircraft in combat. So vital was the path that the Royal Air Force played in the Battle of Britain it inspired the then Prime Minister Winston Churchill to make his immortal speech 'Never in the field of human conflict was so much owed by so many to so few'. That proud tradition remains strong to the present day for the Royal Air Force is second to none. Since September 1993 the training wing of the Royal Air Force has been located at RAF Halton in the county of Buckinghamshire, and it is to here, that the many young men and women come to undertake a seven week intensive training course, to become proud members of the Royal Air Force.*

*We meet CROOKSHANK the enthusiastic new recruit.*

CROOKSHANK: Here I am, Rebecca Jane Crookshank, now H8308183 or just Crookshank or 183 depending on what mood the Corporal's in. I left Plymouth civvie street and train station at 0700 hours with a stinking hangover and awkward farewells from my parents. My Mum and Dad are not talking, zero chat, they're getting a divorce. Mum's been crying *(as her Mum)* 'of course I'm proud of you, I just thought you wanted to do something more creative, more feminine you're so young, my little girl'. Dad, an ex-Royal Marine was the opposite, *(as her Dad)* 'she's old enough to make her own choices, I was sixteen when I joined and only 7.5 stone'. I'll miss them all of course especially my little brother Tom, he looked proper sad waving me off at the station, so I gave him some pocket money to buy himself a pasty, *(she gestures as if speaking down to her little brother, wagging her finger)* a Devon pasty not a Cornish one.

REBECCA: I looked a bit like a pasty, I'd squeezed so much inside my suitcase that I had to wear all my coats at once. It was a challenge choosing what to leave behind.

CROOKSHANK: I really want to join the Royal Marines. Be just like my Dad and my Grandad but I can't because I'm a girl. *(Gesturing to her body.)*

So the RAF it is, I've no fear of flying and my Dad said the food is top notch *(as her Dad)* 'the food is top notch'.

REBECCA: To be honest my choice of service and trade was inspired by the pictures of WRAFs in WW2.

*PROJECTION CLIP: 'PLOTTERS'. Clips of original 1940's female 'plotters' are projected onto the radar screen. She gestures to them.*

Aren't they glamorous? Here they are moving the positions of aircraft on maps with long sticks; 'plotters'. Now Aerospace System Operators, my trade of choice.

CROOKSHANK: While all my friends have gone back to school, here I am. *(Sounds of marching on the camp.)* The camp is like a massive estate. *(She daydreams and takes it all in, playing out the movie in her mind.)* This huge building is called the Officers' Mess, we aren't allowed in there. *(She points to the officers' mess.)*

REBECCA: It was like a grand country estate, a bit like Downton Abbey. Bursting with pride, pomp and circumstance.

CROOKSHANK: The grass airfield is used mainly by light aircraft- gliders, microlights, that sort of thing and the RAF hot air balloon. No time for gliding, I have to get my march on, seven weeks of basic training here I come.

*Sound of a bugle. CROOKSHANK puts on the number one hat adopts a Scottish accent for CPL BUNTING.*

CPL BUNTING: Ladies, welcome to RAF Halton, 'Teach, Learn, Apply'. My name is Cpl Bunting and I will be your drill and training NCO- non-commissioned officer. We will be training you lanky streaks of piss to the highest standard.

If you survive you will contribute to the UK's Defence Strategy both at home and abroad. With equal pay to boot, and ladies let me tell you that's not always been the case.

You will be constantly on the move from medical checks, jabs in the arm, jabs in the arse, haircuts, sit ups, press ups, rope climbs, bleep tests, bulling, cleaning, cleaning, cleaning and no sleep. You will learn how to salute, who to salute and when to 'shut the fuck' up. Which will be most of the time.

The great escape, that's what you wanted isn't it? Wave good bye to your Mummies and Daddies, you're part of a new family now, watch your step and shake your shite.

By the left, quick march.

*She watches the female troop march towards their accommodation.*

HALT. Crookshank. Do you want me to wipe that smile off your face? Get down and give me twenty. *(Beat.)* Women's press ups Crookshank. On your knees.

OK. Ladies, when I demand press ups you get to your knees, understand. Women are not capable of men's press ups. RAF regs. Men on top as they say.

*SOUND CLIP: CROOKSHANK places the hat onto the storage box stage right. She exhausts herself throughout a training montage to music from Top Gun, 'Danger zone'.*

CROOKSHANK: One week in and I've got pecs already. Does that make me unfeminine?

REBECCA: Now I would probably instagram selfies with pride, hashtag fit, hashtag protein shakes, hashtag pecs. I felt muscular, invincible; I thought I was actually in *Top Gun.* *(Beat.)*

CROOKSHANK: I've learnt the NATO phonetic alphabet from Alpha, Bravo, Charlie, to X-ray, Yankee, Zulu. All the non-commissioned ranks, from Aircraftwoman to Warrant Officer, how to iron and starch. Skills for life.

*(She moves to her imagined bed space.)*

Welcome to my bed space. Here's my bed and my one drawer full of cards and pictures.

REBECCA: You weren't allowed anything on display. But where I could, I would find a space for a spot of 'becceration'.

*She moves to CHERYL's bed space.*

CROOKSHANK: I've met some really nice people already. Oh my God there's this one girl, *(as CHERYL who is from Newcastle)* 'Cheryl Baker' she's a trekkie and she actually speaks Klingon. She's been crying all evening cause she misses her pet snake.

REBECCA: Why is it that trekkies always keep reptiles and read Terry Pratchett? We didn't keep in touch.

*She moves to another recruit's bed space.*

CROOKSHANK: There's another girl who has the same actual birthday as me, just seventeen and all. *(As BRIGITTA who has a scouse accent.)* 'Brigitta Bieber' half scouse half German. She drinks tea with every meal and has a serious blushing problem.

*CROOKSHANK becomes 'Brigitta Bieber' (who later is renamed 'Wingwoman') a new recruit with a scouse accent. Introduced by an S Club 7 sound clip. She is sat on the floor reading the instructions from a tin of Brasso.*

WINGWOMAN: Crooky, did you know that Brasso is a metal polish designed to remove tarnish from brass, copper, chrome and stainless steel. It's available either as a liquid or as an 'impregnated wadding pad'. Sounds like a sanitary towel to me. Is Cpl Bunting serious about every bit of brass glistening, even the back of our beret badge? She said she wants to see her face in it. Imagine having that face staring back at ya *(She shudders.)*

Thanks for helping me when I got stuck in me raincoat earlier. You promise not to tell anyone about me blushing problem? It's serious, I have to take pills *(beat)*. This time last year I was on a six day skive bender from school, me head of year said I was destined for the scrap heap. Well fuck you Mr Hatherley, look at me now.

Right, bulling shoes, you get the duster on the finger like so and then pop a bit of polish on it, then you move it in circles over and over, it's like *Blue Peter* isn't it.

Mine don't look as shiny as yours.

Ey, do you reckon Cpl Bunting thinks about frigging herself off when she's bulling her shoes? *(Laughs.)*

*Sound of a drum call to inspection. CROOKSHANK jumps up.*

CROOKSHANK: 0500 hours, inspection due at 0700 hours. Our kits and bed spaces are immaculate. Cpl Bunting keeps calling Brigitta, Biffa like the bin, cause she's a bit shit, but we've worked really hard. There's not a blade of grass on our trainers, kits hung up with military precision with creases that could cut you. We got told that if we all pass we get to have a weekend off.

*Sound of a bugle. CROOKSHANK puts on the number one hat to become CPL BUNTING and inspects the girls marking out three clear spaces for each of the recruits.*

CPL BUNTING: Attention. NO.5 flight. *(Begins inspection.)* Nice Baker. Impressive starching. Good lines. Bedspace check, *(aside to Baker)* in the running for best recruit.

*(To BRIGITTA.)* Right you little Biffa, what's this in here?

*She gestures as if picking up a soap bar.*

Your soap bar soaking wet complete with a pube. Ladies we have enough muff to clog your powder puffs. Aww would you like a cup of suck it the fuck up? Stop blushing for fuck's sake.

*CPL BUNTING walks over to CROOKSHANK's bedspace.*

Crookshank, what's this I spy, a loose thread? Tut tut tut, a nail clipping in your bedspace? Poor drills 183. Ten press ups, down you go, women's press ups, Crookshank.

Looks like you and Biffa have failed the inspection for the flight. Congratulations, no weekend pass. You will spend the weekend doing my ironing. Attention. When I demand attention I expect to hear twenty-five cunts slapping shut. Attention. Better.

*SOUNDCLIP: The Spice Girls 'Wannabe' transport us WINGWOMAN who is ironing in her bedspace talking to CROOKSHANK.*

WINGWOMAN: Before I joined I'd never ironed in me life, me Dad always ironed for us and he taught me how to plait me hair. Iron and starch, iron and starch, at this rate it'll look like rigor mortis has set in. This bit's called the yolk. *(In confidence to CROOKSHANK.)* Crooky, I know you put that nail clipping in your bedspace so it wouldn't just be me who failed the inspection, no one's ever done anything that nice for me before. Thanks ... Oh hang on a minute I've started this the long way round. This shirt's huge, Corporal Bunting's got massive tits.

*Sound of a bugle. CROOKSHANK puts on the NO.1 hat to become CPL BUNTING.*

CPL BUNTING: 183. What's this I hear about you not communicating with your mother? The RAF has a duty of care when you're under eighteen. Get down and give me twenty. Yes women's press ups Crookshank. If you haven't done it by 2200 hours you'll be on jankers duty in the morning. Yes that's right, shovelling shit and pulling weeds from the pavement.

*Lights dim. CROOKSHANK as herself now takes off the hat and looks at it for a moment. She pauses and places it into the backpack stage right.*

*A picture of CROOKSHANK's Mum is projected onto the radar screen. We hear her leave an answerphone message.*

MUM: *(V.O.)* Hi Bec, thank you for your message. Sorry I missed your call, we were out with friends. Um I've got some good news I'm getting married again, I thought it's best coming from me before your Dad and the rest of the town start interfering. Please be happy for me. I've sent you a top up card for your phone. Please call me back soon. Love you always, Mum.

REBECCA: Biffa found me crying in my bedspace and cheered me up with a pepperami. *(Beat.)*

CROOKSHANK: For the last few weeks we've been marching *(she bends down to put on her beret)* down to the regiment to be trained by the RAF Regiment themselves. *(She picks up the rifle.)* The biggest ape men you've ever seen. A lot going on here, here and here, but not a lot going on up here. *(She gestures to her head.)*

*On the firing range. The REGIMENT CORPORAL is training the recruits. Built like an ape he is proudly holding a SA80 rifle. With a*

15

*twinkle in his eye, nothing but dust in his brain and a cockney twang he demonstrates the SA80 capabilities and flirts with CROOKSHANK.*

REGIMENT CPL: Those of you who are still here have passed your NBC, fitness and first aid drills. Currently we are 1 woman and 1, 2, 3, 4, 5 men down. Try to keep up with the girls, lads.

So to clarify, the SA80 'small arms made in the 1980s'. A gift for you Crookshank and your puny small arms also made in the 1980s. It is designed on the ball park principle that the barrel of the weapon goes right the way back into the stock. The result, a short weapon you can fire from a vehicle and is excellent for close quarter combat.

On top of that the sight is far superior than any other Western Army's got, so it's a good weapon. When I was in the field, *(thrusts pelvis)* Operation Desert Storm, an eighteen-year-old rifleman, his first time on the streets, fired 6 rounds in close up environment and he got three kills. So the snapshoot capability is fantastic. In automatic the recoil is really good. It's nice and smooth so you can get good accurate rounds into your target. It's a really good bit of kit.

Right sweethearts. Prone position down. Easy girls. General safety and NSP's GO! Magazine load. READY. Lane one is to fire one 5 round group at the base of figure 11. Lanes 2, 3, 4 and 5 are to fire one 5 round group at the bottom of the white patch. Everybody clear. In your own time go on.

*He watches the recruits open fire. CROOKSHANK removes the beret and gives it a wink. The sound of gunfire is heard. She forgets where she is and tap dances in time with the shots with the rifle, she catches herself out and puts the rifle back on the floor USC.*

CROOKSHANK: I scraped it, by the skin of my teeth I passed my First Aid, Fitness, NBC and Weapons, drills.

Biffa had to re-take her first aid drills cause she ran out of breath and fainted giving mouth to mouth.

REBECCA: We laugh about this now because she's a nurse.

CROOKSHANK: Today we've been in the hangar learning arms drill for our pass out parade. It's like a graduation ceremony. Only two thirds of the recruits have made it through.

REBECCA: One of the lads, Gigsy, was caught in the loading bay putting the rifle to his head. He got taken off the course. 'Temporarily unstable'.

CROOKSHANK: The pass out parade involves intense choreography, shouting and heavy weapons …

It's really painful on the collar bone. But Biffa and I have found a way to make it more comfortable.

*CROOKSHANK reveals a sanitary towel on her shoulder underneath her overalls.*

Giving me wings! *(Beat.)*

It works. I even gave one to trekkie girl and she said thanks in Klingon! Quplah! Which literally means 'success for your forthcoming battle'. *(Sound clip from Star Trek is played.)*

*PROJECTION CLIP: 'PASS OUT PARADE'. Original clips from her 'Pass Out Parade' are projected onto the radar screen. CROOKSHANK changes into her blue overalls. Picks up the rifle and gets ready for the drill commands. At the end of the clip she sees her family and points them out to the audience.*

*Original clip dialogue.*

*PARADE SGT: And in the finest of all theatrical traditions I am the warm up man for this afternoons main event. Now thank you for waiting so patiently for todays proceedings to start. My aim is to take the next few minutes to brief you about the parade format this afternoon. So if I could draw your attention to the programmes you've got where the information that you require is contained. First let me say that we on recruit training squadron are very pleased with the Airmen and Airwomen on parade today in front of you. We set high standards at Halton and all of the young men and women passing out today have shown levels of commitment, determination and teamwork which I suspect they didn't realize they had. We are very pleased with them and you can rightfully be very proud of them.*

CROOKSHANK: That's my Mum in the tartan jacket, my little brother Tom and my Dad with the Royal Marine head. I'm in amongst the parade somewhere in my number ones. It's a bit like *'A Chorus Line'. (She high kicks and spins with the rifle.)*

*Her theatrical day dream is interrupted by the calling of the parade commands, CROOKSHANK demonstrates arms drill. After each command\* she demonstrates the relevant position with the replica rifle.*

DRILL SGT: *(V.O.)* Parade. General Salute.\* Present Arms.\* Slope arms.\* Shoulder Arms.\*

*CROOKSHANK stands with the rifle, it's heavy and it gradually slips throughout the PADRE's speech.*

PADRE: *(V.O.)* Almighty God, we ask you to bless our country, our Queen, and all those who serve our nation in her name. Lord we pray, for all those who serve in the Royal Air Force throughout the world. These airmen and airwomen stand at the gateway of service life. Many have gone before them, and served in the Royal Air Force with dignity and honour. May they follow their good example and be worthy defenders of our nation. Despite the challenges that lie before them, may they endure, and keep their eyes fixed on the promise of reaching the stars. Amen.

CROOKSHANK: Our ladies. *(She puts the rifle down.)*

The pass out parade was mega. We had to perform the parade inside because it was raining so we didn't get to see the flypast, I could hear it though. *(Sound of the Tornado's flying past. CROOKSHANK is captivated.)*

Biffa got the award for most improved recruit. She had to collect it from the commanding officer, in front of the whole parade and *(she tick-tocks to the other side of the stage)* tick-tocked all the way to her award!

My Mum and Dad could barely make eye contact. Mum's got a new name now and it belongs to my Dad's best friend. Biffa and I have new names too: Leading Aircraftwomen. Proud members of the Royal Air Force.

REBECCA: I christened my new found status on the gym mat in the sports hall with the weapons instructor. He made me listen to Savage Garden *(short burst of Savage Garden track)* and he wore JOOP! A quick pump and a squirt.

CROOKSHANK: After basic training we spent a blurry 12 weeks in Newcastle at RAF BOULMER: 'Learn that we may guide' ... training to become Aerospace Systems Operators, ASOPs for short or dopey scopies.

*'What Can I Do' by the Corrs which plays underneath Wingwoman's speech.*

WINGWOMAN: We did it, just. All that radar lingo's gone to my head, blip blip blip.

At least you got a boyfriend though. 'Shorty'; what will your Dad think of him and his size twelve's? All I've got to take home on leave is half a liver and a black eye from that girl in the chicken shop who looked like Baby Spice.

REBECCA: 'Shorty' was our fitness instructor at trade training. 6ft 6 and ten years older than me. He wooed me by taking me to see The Corrs. And drove us down to Norfolk, our next posting in the middle of nowhere.

*SOUND CLIP: A vintage sound clip transports the girls to Neatishead in Norfolk. We meet SQUADRON LEADER WILTON, a female RAF Australian exchange officer. Images of maps and Tornados are projected on the screen behind her. CROOKSHANK puts on rank tabs to become her.*

SQN LDR WILTON: Welcome to RAF Neatishead. Trade group 12 headquarters. *Caelum Tuemur* – 'We watch over the sky'. I believe you will enjoy your time here enormously. Our greatest leader was Air Commodore Joan Hopkins, the first female station commander in the Royal Air Force. Operationally she brought this station to a whole new level of readiness and efficiency. We must continue in her legacy. So how do we do that?

Well, the aim of this Unit is to provide radar, ground-to-air radio and data links coverage in support of national and NATO air defence.

The radar net stretches across NATO countries and is fed by early warning aircraft, ships in the North Sea and coastal stations. The Neatishead bunker can compile a detailed picture of aircraft movements across the whole of Western Europe. You are the unsung heroes and heroines *(she glances to one of the imagined female recruits)* without whom the pilots would be lost.

Every week our air defences are testing capabilities around the northern cape of Norway. The Russians send long range spy planes into international airspace.

If we do not maintain an adequate capability so we can defend ourselves against conventional attack, the probability of use of nuclear weapons from our side to protect ourselves from extremists becomes more likely.

If we ever get to the stage of nuclear war then you, us, the conventional war people, have failed. We are not part of a war machine; we are part of a peace machine. What you see on the screen – simulated or live – is deadly serious.

*CROOKSHANK removes the rank tabs to become herself.*

CROOKSHANK: *(Impressed.)* We have a cool exchange officer called Sqn Ldr Wilton, heading up our squadron down under in the bunker! You great galare. She says she's a 'feminist'.

While all my friends from home finish their A-levels, here I am in Lower Ops. Protecting the UK Air Defence region. Underground. I am a mole and I live in a hole.

*Photographs of the original RAF Neatishead bunker are projected.*

REBECCA: The entrance to the bunker looked like a bungalow. A local woman contacted the police and complained that too many people were stepping off coaches going into a small bungalow, not realizing we were all headed for the

Ops room, defending the skies while she slept safely in her bed.

CROOKSHANK: I'm earning proper wages now. I've even been offered a credit card for £3000. Me and Biffa call ourselves one-day millionaires on pay day.

*Shania Twain 'Man I Feel Like a Woman' underscores WINGWOMAN.*

WINGWOMAN: Champagne lifestyle cider money. *(She chants.)* 'We're all going on an all-day bender. Look out Norwich for the air defenders'. It's gonna be amazing. The lads said you can pay £30 and do this thing called 'The Fridge' where if you succeed in drinking the whole top shelf of bottles – Hooch, WKD, Smirnoff Ice – you get a refund! Get in. Let the challenge commence.

*Jaguars flying past. CROOKSHANK is spellbound.*

CROOKSHANK: Our accommodation, The Block, is 15 miles away at the Jaguar base, RAF Coltishall. 'Aggressive in Defence'. The lads' blocks have cool names like 'Invictus', 'Tornado', 'Spitfire'; ours is called 'Salmon Block'. The WRAF in charge of the block, Senior Aircraft Woman Nicky Bludgell is single, unmarried and nearly thrity-five…

*CROOKSHANK puts on an old bobbly crimson cardigan to become SACW BLUDGELL from Barnsley. She briefs the girls who are lined up at the entrance of the block, pacing up and down to inspect their belongings.*

SACW BLUDGELL: Ladies, new recruits, I am SACW Bludgell and in the block you can call me Chief. You are the new kids on the block, Salmon Block, no jokes about fishy fanny block ye get me? Right open ye bags. Crookshank. What you got in there? Laura Ashley bed linen? That's not regulation. See to it that I have that in my room, ironed and pressed ready for bed change Friday.

Discipline and hierarchy are ingrained in this block. RULES:

1. You will not bring lads back to this block. If there is so much as an Airman's footprint outside there will be punishment, I can assure thee.

21

2. Bull nights. Every week we have bull nights, operation clean-up, spit and spot Mary Poppins style.

3. NO PETS. The last intake of recruits decided to buy a hamster. Wanna know what happened to that? I buried it outside by the bins, with a tea spoon. So NO PETS. And that includes pubic lice, you start itching get yersen to medical centre quick march.

Now piss off. I got to get ready for tonight's station karaoke competition, HEY BIG SPENDER, where I am the face and the voice of the Royal Air Force. I expect standing ovations, whoops and cheers, get them Sambucas lined up at the bar, tonight Matthew I am your star … *(She hums the end of the 'Big Spender' tune as she turns and discards the cardigan.)*

*Now in the ops room CROOKSHANK pushes an ops room stool centre stage which has a headset on it.*

REBECCA: Karaoke aside Bludgell was actually good at her job. *(Beat.)* She trained me to qualify at JAAWSC. Joint Anti-Air Warfare Shore Coordination.

CROOKSHANK: Today it's my turn to train Biffa. The lads say I'm pushy and a kiss ass, it's just cause I'm good at my job. We'll make a great air defence team. I'd trust her with my life. I'm going to call her Wingwoman.

*She puts on the headset sits on the stool centre stage and becomes WINGWOMAN.*

WINGWOMAN: OK. Crooky. Right. So I plug my headset in. Open the authentication manual. Switch on VHF 1 & 2.

Secure comms line for us and the Navy.

*WINGWOMAN gestures, as if to press the comms channels.*

But I'm not actually gonna press it cause this is training obviously. OK. So, a three letter authentication code for the Navy to authenticate …

*She pretends to press the comms channel button.*

HMS Illustrious are you receiving over, receiving over.

HMS Illustrious, this is Neatishead, authenticate Tango India Tango over. *(Beat.)* What? It was just an example.

The Navy line up the letters and boom, they will authenticate the corresponding code in the manual.

What if the code doesn't correspond? *(Beat.)* We all die? Shut up you dick. *(Beat.)* Can my codename be Wingwoman? That's dead cool. Much better than Biffa.

HMS Illustrious, this is the smouldering sexy Wingwoman.

November Oscar Bravo. Authenticate November Oscar Bravo over. Imagine if they came back with Charlie Uniform Mike. Brilliant.

*PROJECTION CLIP: 'RADAR 1.' Lights down. original photos of Rebecca in uniform, in fatigues, her daily routine, going out with the girls and her mother getting re-married, are projected for the first radar sequence. Sounds of radar sweeps and archived footage play for thrity-five seconds.*

REBECCA: The girls on squadron were like my new family. Bludgell was well on side, still nicked my bed linen but she turned a blind eye to our underage drinking antics.

*(As BLUDGELL.)* 'Old enough to fire a gun old enough to drink.'

CROOKSHANK: Now we're eighteen and tonight it's mine and Wingwoman's joint party at the NAAFI.

*CROOKSHANK changes into a pink shell suit top. 'Spice Up Your Life' by the Spice Girls is played. She dances through her Birthday Montage. Becoming increasingly intoxicated she finds it difficult to hold herself up. As the music and her experience distorts, she moves into the audience, picks out a male and passes out on his lap. It's the next morning she realizes what she's done and that she's late.*

CROOKSHANK: Oh fuck. I think I pulled one of the engineers from the Jaguar Squadron. *(She gets back to the stage.)*

Shorty will never know ...

REBECCA: You know the 6ft 6 guy who wooed me by taking me to see the Corrs? We were still a thing.

CROOKSHANK: Shit, I'm gonna miss the transport for my annual appraisal. Squaddie shower.

REBECCA: After a year of service you automatically received a promotion, a third propeller.

*Sound of tornados in the distance.*

CROOKSHANK: Senior Aircraftwoman Crookshank. While all my friends from school are on their gap year, I'm in Upper Ops. The bigger picture. I sit on console with the Weapons Controllers, book the air space and liaise with Air Traffic Control.

*SOUND CLIP: A vintage sound clip is played. CROOKSHANK puts on rank tabs to become SQN LDR WILTON.*

SQN LDR WILTON: SACW Crookshank. Take a seat for your annual appraisal. I've observed a great aptitude in your work and commitment to trade group 12. I think you should consider going for your commission, training to become an officer like Air Commodore Joan Hopkins, the first female station commander. If you'd just like to review your comments, and sign here. *(Beat.)* You're going to have a lot more time on your hands what with SACW Bieber away ...

Oh we've posted her to HMS Illustrious, an exchange tour with the Royal Navy.

*Now on the ship. WINGWOMAN is introduced by the sound of a ship's horn. She sits on the military storage boxes. Her feet dangle as if she is sat on the top bunk.*

WINGWOMAN: Crooky, here I am safe and sound on HMS Illustrious, 'Lusty' for short. I know it's shit I didn't say a proper goodbye but I know what you're like at the end of Armageddon so I didn't want a drama. Least you'll have more time to spend with Shorty? As soon as I wrote that, I filled up. But I'll be fine once we hit the first port of call, Gibraltar, and I hit the bottle.

Right now it's like a ghost ship. There's a ship's company photo on the flight deck, but I'm having a fat day and me in my RAF cap would stick out like a sore thumb. Write soon, Wingwoman.

CROOKSHANK: So we are split formation.

*Sounds of distant tornados in flight.*

It's quite fun writing to one another and messaging each other on ASMA.

REBECCA: ASMA was like instant messaging but on an old brown Acorn computer with a black screen and green flashing cursor. *(She spots a more mature member of the audience.)* Remember those?

CROOKSHANK: My job's getting even more exciting now. I've moved up from Weapons Controllers' Assistant to trainee Fighter Allocator Assistant.

*Sounds of the ops room. CROOKSHANK is watching the radar and listens to comms over the headset. CROOKSHANK sits on the ops room stool as and stands when becoming SQN LDR WILTON.*

CROOKSHANK: Ma'am, we have an X-ray over the Northern Cape. Buchan just rang and reported that their radar has been destroyed; mass raid has broken through in Juliet Juliet high level heading west. The track production officer downstairs, Ma'am, is reporting a loss of comms and picture on the Northern radar sweep.

SQN LDR WILTON: We need to start moving rapidly. All hell has broken loose on the continent. We've warning of another large raid coming in across Germany most of which has broken through. I want all QRA at readiness 10 and bring the rest up to a high state.

CROOKSHANK: Calling Coningsby now Ma'am. Coningsby, this is Neatishead: all aircraft readiness ten. Tracker 1, extend your area. Ma'am, the TPO said we are going to need more fighters.

SQN LDR WILTON: Just check with the TPO to make sure there's nothing else coming behind. Master controller, I'm launching all aircraft. Coningsby all aircraft scramble scramble scramble.

*Images of a QRA scramble are projected on the screen.*

TANNOY: *(V.O.)* ENDEX ENDEX ENDEX

SQN LDR WILTON: Nice work one Squadron. Stand down. Rest assured your air space is safe. *(Beat.)* Debrief at 2300 hours.

Quick work, Crookshank. We make a good team. You remind me of Joan or 'Aunty Joan' as she is known. *(She notices CROOKSHANK is in a daze.)* Crookshank, earth to Crookshank? You don't want to be an assistant all your career; you could be a specialist fighter controller officer like me and Air Commodore Joan Hopkins, the first female station commander. So quit daydreaming. Seriously, you should think about going for that commission.

*CROOKSHANK receives an answer phone message from her DAD. A picture of him in his Royal Marine uniform is projected on the screen. CROOKSHANK is not lit. She moves the stool back to USC.*

DAD: *(V.O.)* Hi, Bec, this is your Dad. Um, call us back when you can. Grandma died today. You're going to need to book some leave. Me and Grandad think you should wear your number ones. Love you.

*Sound of a ship's horn.*

WINGWOMAN: Crooky, sorry to hear about your Grandma. But look on the bright side, you did well in the simex, maybe you should go for your commission?

Oh, we're in Al Jabyl. Me and Tina, one of the WREN's had to go out all covered up cause we are women. So I wore a fleece and tracky bottoms in thirty-seven degree heat and nearly boiled to death.

On Sunday we get to Abu Dhabi and we are going to watch Bobby Davro on the beach so that will be good. I tried to phone you but think you're on nights.

CROOKSHANK: So my Grandma is brown bread. She was Irish, I know everyone has an Irish Grandma but I really have, *(beat)* did. She was suffering from Alzheimer's; called out for my Grandad and died just like that. Not even a blip on the radar. *(Beat.)*

*Sound of Tornados, CROOKSHANK continues as herself as if in a trance.*

The Tornado, is one of the very few aircraft in the world that is able to operate at low level, day or night and in poor weather.

*She snaps out of her trance.*

REBECCA: I was grounded, facilitating aircraft, to fly supersonic, defend and destroy. I couldn't feel my wings. But for the first time, I felt the weight of what I was trained to do. *(Beat.)*

CROOKSHANK: The family home is for sale. Dad and his new wife are moving to Scotland to be nearer to my Grandad. To top it all off I got the news that I have an STD.

*She throws a look at the member of the audience she sat on previously.*

All treatable, perks of free military medical care, top notch like the food. I'm not telling Shorty, he'll get sus and that will be the end of us.

*Sound of a ship's horn.*

WINGWOMAN: Crooky, guess what, I got laid, yes me I got laid! It's a bit awkward as he's equivalent of a Sgt, so strictly out of bounds. Oh by the way, we are in Abu Dhabi. The scenery is great as is the architecture but the people are well weird.

We're leaving soon on our way to Bahrain for more boozing. Tina can neck a bottle of Hooch in five seconds. I bet she could do 'The Fridge', she's worse than Bludgell.

*PROJECTION CLIP: 'RADAR 2'. Projections of original photos of Rebecca's family, daily work activities, social occasions and her father getting re-married sweep the screen accompanied by radar sounds.*

*Sound of a ship's horn.*

WINGWOMAN: Crooky, you know the other PTI from trade training? Shorty's mate? Well he joined the ship at Abu Dhabi. I'm not really sure how to put this. Shorty's a fucking shitbag. He's got a wife in Leicester, a cottage, and he shops for wallpaper at the weekends for fuck's sake. I wonder if she's got an STD and all. Oh my god, Tina is amazing! We organised a fete, it was really good. We're pretty much nowhere, I'm just snatching a sun bathe on the flight deck. Things can only get better. Miss you loads. Wingwoman.

CROOKSHANK: I confronted Shorty about his civvie wife. I've chucked the pager he gave me and I'm ignoring all comms, from him and Wingwoman. The only she's good for is a slap in the face. She's probably too busy out with Tina anyway.

REBECCA: I didn't slap her, she was on a ship stuck in the middle east for fucks sake but I planned it out in my head, played it through in slow motion. I was only 18.

CROOKSHANK: Tonight I'm out at the NAAFI another karaoke sing off for Bludgell, this time some civvies are involved.

*CROOKSHANK puts on BLUDGELL's cardigan to become her. BLUDGELL is waiting for her winning announcement.*

ANNOUNCEMENT: *(V.O.)* And the winner of tonight's karaoke is Sarah from the Spar shop with her version of 'Love Lift Me Up Where You Belong'.

BLUDGELL: *(Gutted, to CROOKY.)* Two more Sambucas. Line 'em up girlfriends. *(To SARAH.)* Right, Sarah, I might not be the face or the voice but I'm a fucking Airwoman at that.

The minute you walked in the joint, I could see you were a big fat tosser … eeee, yey have some of that. *(Bludgell gestures as if to masturbate like a man towards Sarah.)*

Come on Crooky, I can be your Wingwoman now. Shots shots shots shots, eeee.

Down in one. That's my girl. *(She notices a pint glass on the bar and shouts to SARAH.)* Just cause we got fannies don't mean we can't piss in a pint glass.

*(To CROOKSHANK.)* Watch and learn. *(Centre stage, hovering over the imagined pint glass, we hear sounds of urination.)* Never let your vulva dangle in the dust.

*The next morning. CROOKSHANK tries to wake up BLUDGELL.*

CROOKSHANK: Bludgell, we're gonna miss the transport. Bludgell, wake up. Right I'm coming in. Blu …

*CROOKSHANK enters SACW BLUDGELL's room and sees the horrific image of her death, she is laying in her own vomit. Sounds of sirens. Her cardigan is centre stage. She picks up the cardigan tenderly and carries it like a coffin to 'The Last Post' finally laying it stage right in memorial (Beat.)*

PADRE: *(V.O.) (The PADRE whistles every time he vocalises the 's' sound.)* SACW BLUDGELL. A committed, strong and sincere member of the Royal Air Force. An ambassador for the entertainments committee, with a voice of an angel. Taken too soon. Let us celebrate her life and legacy, with the gift of faith and the blessing of peace. We will remember her. Through Jesus Christ our Lord, Amen.

CROOKSHANK: Our Ladies.

*She salutes. (Beat.) Sound of a ship's horn. WINGWOMAN shares a series of updates, increasingly frustrated by the lack of response from CROOKSHANK.*

WINGWOMAN: Crooky, when they told me on the ship I nearly passed out. Choking on her own puke, horrendous. I bet you don't want your Laura Ashley bed linen back now.

I haven't got any good news, I'm just getting more and more depressed. The ship's company have had a drinking ban for a week. I was supposed to be in Bahrain but the winds are too strong and to top it off I've got red patches on my face where I've missed bits with the sun cream. So I'm sitting in my cabin listening to Shania Twain. Heartbroken to fuck, Wingwoman.

*Sound of a ship's horn.*

WINGWOMAN: Crooky. The pyramids were brilliant! The ship got stuck in the canal, so we stayed in a hotel and me and Tina cracked open the gin and got hammered. You've obviously forgotten how to write. Hopefully still yours, Wingwoman.

*Sound of a ship's horn.*

WINGWOMAN: Am I a complete loser? Am I fugly? Do I have no personality? I haven't heard from you in ages. Out of sight out of mind eh.

I've got some news, not that you could give two hoots. Mike. Oh my God he's lush. Me and Mike stayed up till 0300 hours, all we did was chat and hold hands, it was dead nice.

Tina reckons he's well into me. Please write soon. Wingwoman.

*SOUND CLIP: A vintage sound clip takes us back to the bunker. SQN LDR WILTON is downbeat and concerned about CROOKSHANK.*

SQN LDR WILTON: Take a seat, Crookshank. *(Beat.)* There's a collective concern about your work, appearance and bearing. I know it's been a struggle for us all here on squadron since the passing of SACW Bludgell. However, I am withdrawing my recommendation for your commission at this present time. *(Beat.)* Chin up, things can only get better.

*CROOKSHANK rips open her overalls and exits stage right. An answer machine message from her little brother TOM is played.*

TOM: *(V.O.)* Bec, it's Tom. Dad's sold the house already. Now I have to choose to live with Mum or Dad. It's OK for you, fucking off before the shit hit the fan. As soon as I'm sixteen I'm joining up. There's fuck all to do in Devon or Glasgow. Miss you, blister, call me.

*PROJECTION CLIP:'RADAR 3' projections of photos of her Grandmas coffin, painkillers and alcohol sweep the screen underscored by sirens. CROOKSHANK has overdosed. She exits and changes backstage into a surreal dress, made from a sequined Union Jack flag and camouflage corset. JOAN HOPKINS appears in CROOKSHANK'S imagined reality. She is the spirit guide of JOAN HOPKINS, there's a hint of 'glinda' the good witch about her.*

JOAN HOPKINS: Senior Aircraftwoman Crookshank. *(Beat.)* You're in the Norfolk and Norwich Hospital. No need to salute. You need your rest.

Let me introduce myself. Air Commodore Joan Hopkins, yes, the first female station commander in the Royal Air Force. We need to have a heart to heart. You nearly took your own life and why would you do such a thing? We both know you can be bright, hard-working and focussed. When you're not fantasizing of course. You had a promising career ahead of you, you could have made a fine officer, spread your wings, flown up through the ranks. But perhaps that's not what you want?

What do you want, Crookshank? Something more creative? We've all been there, too afraid to go after what we really want. But you should never stop trying. Sometimes we feel we are alone, but we are not. It's at times like these I think about *(beat)* penguins. I think about them very deeply, many of my close friends are penguins. Penguins are a naturally curious and inquisitive species. They build their nests on rocky edges and bounce from ledge to ledge. On land penguins can look funny and clumsy. However, when penguins are in the water they transform, they are graceful, aerodynamic, and exquisite.

Let me tell you a little story. When penguins jump into the water they are at risk from predators; killer whales, sea lions, sharks, oh my. But one penguin has to be brave, take the leap and be the first penguin to venture into the dark waters. Dive in despite the dangers. Do you copy Crookshank?

If you choose a military career you will always be the third penguin, after your father and grandfather. If you follow your instincts and pursue another calling, you will be the first penguin. The end.

You've looked death in the eye, Crookshank. There's no way I intend to lose you now. Fear of failure can paralyse you, embracing the unfamiliar can make you feel alive. Think outside the box, Crookshank.

Here's a gift. *(Magical sound, she gives a toy penguin to CROOKSHANK.) (Beat.)* To remind you to bounce, bounce back like a penguin. You'll need company for your next mission.

Oh, you're hallucinating; I am in your head. The penguin is real, your parents left it for you. They care about you very much.

Remember, it's not how hard you hit, it's how hard you get hit and keep moving forwards. Remember the RAF motto;

*Per ardua ad astra* – through adversity to the stars...

*CROOKSHANK steps out of the dress. With her overalls tied at the waist she looks at the JOAN HOPKINS hat as she takes it off and thoughtfully places it on top of the discarded JOAN HOPKINS dress.*

REBECCA: I was feeling sorry for myself. I'd gone out to do 'The Fridge'. Didn't beat the lads came home and cried like a baby. Took as many painkillers as I could get my hands on and watched the film *Sliding Doors* until I passed out.

My tribe had upstaged me. I felt like I wanted to disappear forever, stop squawking emergency and turn the lights out, for good. I wanted to eject myself from the underground bunker and fly fast off the edge of the runway. Everything felt smaller, tighter, even my shoes. It was hard to breathe. I'd made a commitment to my heritage but the more I questioned the role of what I was doing the more I unravelled my heart and it hurt. I only wanted to be part of something, find a new family, something strong to hold me. But I'd reached a dark destination and I could only make out shadows, people's voices then blue lights closing in. So stupid.

I was sent back to Salmon Block it was all the same but different. I was medically downgraded, offered Prozac and some counselling sessions with the Padre. *(Beat.)*

*(She pulls up her overalls and fastens them.)* Now we've landed in the bit of the story where I get my shit together. Survival. I want to be the first penguin. I *can* be the first penguin. Thank you Air Commodore Joan Hopkins, Ma'am, I salute you.

*Sound of a ship's horn.*

WINGWOMAN: Crooky, you dingbat. I'm glad you are feeling better, it was so good to hear your voice over the phone. Everything's gone Pete Tong since we've been apart. I got absolutely minging the other night, danced on the podium, fell off. Thought I'd gone overboard; and I think I may have kissed Tina, on the lips.

Seeing you hit rock bottom like that has made me realize that I want to help people. Make a difference.

Today we went to Jerusalem, and to tell the truth it was a bit tacky and expensive. I can't wait to see you. Your Wingwoman, for keeps.

*SOUND CLIP: A vintage sound clip takes us back to the bunker CROOKSHANK puts on the rank tabs to become SQN LDR WILTON.*

SQN LDR WILTON: Crookshank, take a seat. Here in the Royal Air Force we are committed to getting you back on the road to recovery. We understand that you were dealing with a considerable amount of personal battles. But I am delighted to see you're moving forwards. We think a change of scenery would do you good. A posting to an operational environment will enhance your experience as an Airwoman. We're sending you to the South Atlantic, the Falkland Islands.

*CROOKSHANK puts on a camouflage jacket, on top of her overalls. She sits on the ops stool centre stage with the penguin as if inside the aircraft.*

*PROJECTION: 'TRISTAR TAKES OFF FROM BRIZE NORTON'.*

CROOKSHANK: Well here we are, me and Penguin Joan. All strapped in for an eighteen hour flight. This is a Tristar, it's like a big tin can. We get to stop over at Ascension Island, where I get a stamp in my passport and a whole free can of Budweiser.

The Falkland Islands. I wonder what it's going to be like. If Jim Davidson comes out to entertain the troops, I might actually kill myself. *(Covering the penguins ears.)* Joking. I can't wait to see the penguins.

*CROOKSHANK now settled on the Falkland Islands goes on the penguin tour led by guide SANDY. CROOKSHANK puts on a practical beige rain mac to become SANDY, a well-spoken, hardy, out-doorsy woman.*

SANDY: Listen up, it's bloody windy. Come in closer, yes that's right. So I'm Sandy your guide today, proud to be a ninth generation Falkland Islander. The Falkland Islands is a self-sufficient country with a long history and unique culture.

Here comes the hail, don't worry it will be over in the flashest of flashes.

The Falkland Islanders are peaceful, hard-working and resilient people. See, I told you it would stop.

Our society is thriving and forward-looking. Look at it, it's half the size of bloody Wales. Glorious. Onwards!

Here's what you've all been waiting for, the penguin colony. This is one of the world's greatest penguin capitals: as many as a million penguins nest in the Falklands every summer. As you can see the male penguin sits on the egg while the females go out to forage for food; progressive little so and so's aren't they.

*(The Falkland Islands National Anthem underscores.)* People always ask me where I was during the Falklands War and I know you're dying to find out. Well, my husband and I were on an expedition in the Outer Hebrides when the Argentinians invaded. I obviously got whiff of what was happening and contacted the MOD immediately as I had in my possession my personal slide collection. Years of photographs of the topography of the islands, the flora and fauna, information I knew would be essential to reclaim the islands from the Argentines. Of course the MOD sent for me immediately and without my personal slide collection we would not have won the war. I guess that's what one would call a Kodak moment! Onwards ...

*CROOKSHANK puts on her headset. The sound of tornados can be heard.*

CROOKSHANK: Ops cabin RAF Mount Pleasant 'Protect the right'. It's a more basic version of my job back at the Neatishead bunker, but I'm above ground at least.

There's a radio station here, British Forces Broadcasting Services – BFBS. I'm paying them a visit on my day off, instead of getting pissed.

*SOUND CLIP: Original sound clips from CROOKSHANK's radio show are played. She sits on the ops stool as if in the radio studio.*

Becca Crookshank, BFBS. Oh, hi, I didn't see you there! Radio joke! So tonight's entertainment, the cyber café, is open till 9 P.M. The Bowl of course open till late serving the legendary garlic and tomato calzones, Snakebites 2-4-1 and penguin racing. *(Sound clips from Radio Gaga are played, originally from clip of Tornado F3s.)* This next track goes out to the Tornado squadron, ripping it up in the crew room ...

My own freaking radio show. It's going down a storm. I'm like a local celeb on the Island. I've been making deals with the Tornado squadron, I play their song requests and they fly low over the station. *(Sounds of Tornados flying over the station, she's captivated.)*

*Run DMC's 'Christmas in Hollis' is played.*

Good morning Mount Pleasant and Merry Christmas. That was a shout out for everyone on shift today. Looking forward to the Ops squadron dining in night, officers serving up our Christmas dinner, keep it clean.

Sadly this is my last show *(radio BOO clip)* before I'm off to a remote radar site for the final weeks of my detachment – Affirmative four weeks on Mount Alice. Merry Christmas to me.

Thanks so much team BFBS, you've been incredible, letting me send out my love over the airwaves. This next track goes out to everyone on duty on heliops in the morning. *(Helicopter sound.)* 0700 hours please don't dick about in the airspace, precious cargo. *(She moves her gaze and shifts her weight as if inside the helicopter.)*

My first time on a helicopter, it's quite cool, seeing the island from up here is wicked.

*PROJECTION CLIP: 'ALICE WAVE' Lads' banter can be heard. Men are lined up mooning on the helipad this is an original clip.*

Look there's the helipad and they've all come out to greet me. What the fuck, twenty-eight assholes.

REBECCA: Literally, twenty-eight blokes mooning me in. That, my friends, is what you call the Alice wave.

*Sound of a ship's horn.*

WINGWOMAN: Dearest Crook, hopefully by the time you get this you will know the situation. My tour has been extended. We're going to a top secret location. Sierra Leone. Shh. *(Beat.)*

But we have to crack on. Hopefully I won't die. Thanks for the tapes from your radio show, I'll be listening to them on my Walkman. Good luck on Mount Alice. *(Beat.)*

*CROOKSHANK introduces the audience to her bed space.*

CROOKSHANK: Welcome to my new bed space. It's in a portacabin with the twenty-eight arseholes. I'm the only girl. I've made it quite cosy, lots of pictures on the wall, my new personal issue Laura Ashley bed linen. I'm making a little film to send to home my Mum but the lads keep swearing and filming footage of their turds.

*PROJECTION CLIP: 'Turd Trials' An original clip of one of the lads filming his turd in the toilet.*

*Original clip dialogue.*

*LAD: Here we have a stool. Watch it go. You're watching the 'Trials of Alice' (the turd is flushed away). Becca, I'm no longer full of shit.*

*End of clip.*

CROOKSHANK: Today we can't go outside cause it's too windy. So I'm having my initiation ceremony instead.

*CROOKSHANK becomes MOUNT ALICE MAN. A young lad stuck on the mountain for too long. Angry, bullish who enjoys the ritual of the initiation ceremony.*

MOUNT ALICE MAN: Welcome Crookwank, are you ready for the rubber chicken. EEEEEE. A little rubber slap to the cheek, oh she's a blusher, but is she a gusher? Oi, Taff, get your kit off, show her your moobs. Titwank on all fours for the teabag treat!

*He bounces up and down as if his testicles bounce off the back of CROOKSHANK's neck chanting …*

Teabag, teabag, teabag.

REBECCA: I got to sit in the bar, where the choices of drinks were Stella or Stella, while the lads manhandled me wearing nothing but rubber gloves.

*PROJECTION CLIP: 'INITIATION CEREMONY'. Three original photos from CROOKSHANK's initiation are projected. The men are naked apart from rubber gloves on their genitals. CROOKSHANK fully clothed, is put into starfish shapes to the humour of the men.*

REBECCA: *(She gestures to the clip.)* Honestly you couldn't write it. While all my friends from home are at University. Here I am.

*Gesturing to her picture on the screen, she is upside down being manhandled by naked service men.*

REBECCA: This fine specimen of a human being *(she points to one of the men)*, was married with three daughters. It occurred to me that my experience as a woman in this environment was different to that of my Dad's. I wondered if he had ever been teabagged?

*PROJECTION CLIP: 'MOUNT ALICE BANTER'. Original video clips of CROOKSHANK and the lads on the mountain site. CROOKSHANK settles into her operations cabin and prepares for communications.*

*Original clip dialogue.*

*CROOKSHANK: I don't want any swearing.*

*LAD1: What, so you can't say fuck?*

*LAD2: Bollocks.*

*LAD1: You can't say fucking shit?*

*CROOKSHANK: This is for my Mum!*

*(Laughter.)*

*LAD1: Say hello to your Mum Becs (Lad 2 pulls a moonie in the background.)*

*CROOKSHANK: Hello.*

*LAD 1: Ha-ha. Hello Becca's Mum. This is a rock on Mount Alice, wait –*

*LAD 2: Right, get in get in get in. Yesss.*

*LAD 1: Is she up for a gang bang?*

*LAD 1: This is Bec's pussy.*

*CROOKSHANK: This is Tigger, (CROOKSHANK is pointing to the station's cat) we've just found, can you just-*

*LAD 1: It's got a trigger. (He keeps trying to touch CROOKSHANK.)*

*CROOKSHANK: Now look what you've done, you've just ruined it.*

*LAD 1: It's only a fucking cat woman!*

*LAD 2: Fucking pussy.*

*CROOKSHANK: CUT, CUT now!*

*LAD 2: That is a fucking pussy!*

*LAD 1: Howez Bec's just do us a favour and open your legs We're not filming. Honestly, lay down and open your legs*

*CROOKSHANK: I'm not stupid.*

*LAD 1: Lay down and open your legs. Put this in … (He is holding an extendable phallic metal tool of some kind.)*

*CROOKSHANK: That's horrible.*

*LAD 1: Honestly, open your knees.*

*CROOKSHANK: Can you just be nice?*

*End of clip.*

*It's NYE. Sounds of 'Auld Lang Syne' underscore. Both CROOKSHANK and WINGWOMAN are working and connect over the airwaves. It's a sad moment for CROOKSHANK, she is missing home terribly and knows that she needs support.*

CROOKSHANK: Ops cabin. Mount Alice. My job is pretty much the same as on the Main Island except it's in a portacabin. I call it my hide out.

*She sits to communicate over the comms to the ship.*

HMS Illustrious this is Mike Papa Alpha over.

WINGWOMAN: *(V.O.)* Mike Papa Alpha authenticate Tango India Tango over.

CROOKSHANK: Authenticating standby. Romeo Juliet Charlie. Authenticate November Oscar Bravo over.

WINGWOMAN: *(V.O.)* Authenticating standby. Charlie Uniform Mike. Over. *(Beat.)*

CROOKSHANK: Wingwoman. *(She is overjoyed.)*

WINGWOMAN: *(V.O.)* Crooky.

CROOKSHANK: Location over?

WINGWOMAN: *(V.O.)* We are nowhere. Over.

CROOKSHANK: Ditto. Missingness. Over.

WINGWOMAN: *(V.O.)* Ditto. 10, 9, 8, 7, 6,

TOGETHER: 5, 4, 3, 2, 1. *(CROOKSHANK unable to speak the first few numbers, joins WINGWOMAN at NO. 5, drawing on every bit of remaining strength.)*

CROOKSHANK: Happy New Year, Wingwoman. Over.

WINGWOMAN: *(V.O.)* Happy New Year. Sgt Intercepting. TTFN out.

CROOKSHANK: Over and out.

*The music climaxes. Sounds of festive joy. CROOKSHANK clearly struggling, is interrupted by the lads knocking at the door. She becomes MOUNT ALICE MAN.*

MOUNT ALICE MAN: Crookwank, what you doing in there? Open the fucking door, I wanna put my dick in you *(Laughs.)* If you don't come out I'll throw rocks at the sheep. Taff, she's crying. Crooky, we were only having a laugh, Aaaahhhhhhhh fuckin' titwank you fucking lesbian. *(Beat.)*

REBECCA: I took to keeping an eye on the sheep and I formed a 'tactical' relationship with one of the Army signallers. It worked, well the night time door knocking soon died down.

*PROJECTION CLIP: 'REBECCA'S BED SPACE' original video clips of CROOKSHANK in her room with one of the Lads, from her home movie are played. HearSay is playing in the background.*

*Original clip dialogue.*

CROOKSHANK: *What?*

LAD: *What do you want me to ask you?*

CROOKSHANK: *This is my bedroom at Alice (The camera pans to show the portacabin accommodation.)*

LAD: *She's not in here much, she's normally in mine.*

CROOKSHANK: *Please just for five minutes of your life can you be serious?*

LAD: *I'm always serious when I'm rogering you ... Sorry Becs, I'm sorry.*

CROOKSHANK: *Can we start this again?*

LAD: *Go!*

CROOKSHANK: *Ask me some questions about Alice, not rude, that are suitable for family viewing.*

LAD: *Have you enjoyed your time at Alice?*

CROOKSHANK: *Yes, thank you.*

LAD: *Why?*

CROOKSHANK: *Ah, I can't be bothered, stop it. Turn it off now.*

*End of clip.*

*PROJECTION CLIP: 'Measles'. Original clips of CROOKSHANK filming 'Measles'. Intense sounds of tornados in flight.*

CROOKSHANK: Twice a week we have operational training for the Tornado squadron, it's called Measles. The Tornado F3s creep up the side of the mountain in formation flying low, the whole station shakes, vibrates; it's brilliant. Variable sweep-wing combat aircraft. On radar we identify them as interceptors. They launch in pairs and are operated by a pilot and a navigator.

*Original clip dialogue from CROOKSHANK.*

*CROOKSHANK: Wowsers.*

CROOKSHANK: *(Shouts over the sounds of the Tornados.)* It's a proper powerful sensation, like I forget where I am, where I want to be, everything. For a moment I feel I can do anything. I'm supersonic, invincible, I'm me, my voice can break the sound barrier and everyone can hear me. *(Beat.)*

Comms with Wingwoman are more frequent now. We're emailing, I set up this new thing called a hotmail account.

*Sounds of 1990's internet dial up tones. WINGWOMAN is back in the UK, waiting patiently for the dial-up to complete.*

WINGWOMAN: Dearest Crook, I'm back in Blighty, look at me sending emails. I thought a lot about what you said about being the first penguin and I've decided I'm going to be a nurse. All my paperwork's ready and as soon as you get back we can put our papers in together. I'm doing the venders on my break to pass the shift; I've got 30p left, will it be the buttons or the skips? Decisions. Counting every hour to our new lives. Wingwoman.

CROOKSHANK: Time is standing still on the mountain. We don't even have a vending machine. So I've made up my own version of 'Treasure Hunt'. The lads are helping me by planning the clues.

*PROJECTION CLIP: 'INITIATION'. 'Treasure hunt'. Original video clips of CROOKSHANK and the lads playing 'Treasure Hunt'. Sounds of running and strong winds on the mountain.*

*Original Clip Dialogue.*

*LAD: Stop the clock, stop the clock, OK. It's big and round like your fanny all gagged and bound.*

*In the clip CROOKSHANK is running in a high viz jacket. The lads throw stones at her. She's giggling.*

*CROOKSHANK: Where is it? Where is it? Is it the radar?*

*LAD: Keep running woman.*

> *She falls off the path. Cut to the next clue.*

*LAD: Aneka the bike Crookshank, this place is never used but you can get a prick in it?*

> *More shots of CROOKSHANK running in a high viz jacket. She finds herself in the medical centre cabin.*

*CROOKSHANK: Ah, am I warm?*

*LAD: Mmm are you warm, we could arrange that.*

> *CROOKSHANK spots a file on the computer screen.*

*CROOKSHANK: Ah treasure hunt!*

> *She clicks the file and a new page opens to reveal 'WE WANT TO FUCK YOUR MUM' in capital letters. They all laugh including CROOKSHANK. End of clip.*

> *Sound of the door knocking. REBECCA becomes MOUNT ALICE MAN who continues to harass CROOKSHANK.*

> *Tricking his way into her room*

MOUNT ALICE MAN: Crookshank open up, they need you on radar to guide in the Chinook with the supply drop.

Wahh you gullible little slut.

*(He sees the penguin.)* Ahh, what we got here, a cuddly toy? This doesn't look like RAF issue, does it Taff. There's no room for cuddly toys or silly little girls in the military ...

Quick, Taff. Cable tie her.

REBECCA: *(To audience.)* I was in full uniform. It could have been worse, I know this. I also now know how to escape cable ties from Google. According to the art of manliness dot com, there are three ways;

1. 'Slipping out' simply present your hands to your captor with fists clenched and palms facing down.

2. 'Breaking Zip ties' tighten the ties with your teeth, the tighter the cable tie the easier it is to break. Lift your hands above your head and bring them down to your stomach quickly flaring your elbows out like chicken wings.

3. 'Shimming out' Defeat the mechanism of the zip tie with some sort of shim. You can use a variety of objects to lift the locking bar: a finger nail, a pin, even a credit card. This method is easier with multiple people held captive together, but I was on my own.

*MOUNT ALICE MAN is holding her penguin like an oscar.*

MOUNT ALICE MAN: And the winner of the drama queen award goes to Crookshank. Come and get it …

*MOUNT ALICE MAN destroys the penguin toy to System of the Down 'Bounce' ripping out it's stuffing. Strobe lighting is used.*

CROOKSHANK: *(Clearing up the penguin stuffing.)* I told my Flight Sgt I wanted to Foxtrot Oscar off Mount Alice. They sent the Commanding Officer up by helicopter. No Alice Wave for him.

We will be dealing with the personnel accordingly, that's what the Commanding Officer said. He insisted on having the meeting in my bedroom, because there was nowhere else to go. He looked like a mole, I asked him if he liked my Laura Ashley bed linen. He said that if I kept my mouth shut and stuck out the rest of the tour I wouldn't get a bad report and he could arrange a flight for me *(beat)*, in a Tornado F3…

REBECCA: I remember the pause for thought. I could still hear 'Pure and Simple' by Hearsay playing through my headphones. He could only have been twenty-four. In charge of troops, nipping things in the bud before *(Beat.)* … I imagined myself taking it right to the top, to someone maybe in their thirties less mole-like. I saw myself standing outside the Supreme Court, wearing a black suit, dark glasses and saying no comment. On trial and triumphant, people actually listening to me. And then I felt I couldn't swallow, I felt the weight of loyalty, heritage, pride, fear and fatigue. *(Beat.)* I said I would stick it out. I didn't want a bad report. I took the flight in the Tornado. *(Beat.)*

In 2001 I decided to leave the Royal Air Force. If I'd stayed in I'd be due to retire in five years with a pension. But I didn't and here I am. *(She takes off her camo jacket.)* With courage, determination and resilience to pursue another calling.

*CROOKSHANK puts on a sequined camouflaged jacked with toy soldiers on the shoulders, very like the JOAN HOPKINS dress.*

Spreading my wings. Something more creative. Become the first penguin.

*Per ardua ad astra* – through adversity to the stars…

*An original picture of CROOKSHANK in her flying suit next to the Tornado F3 with the pilot is projected. She turns to look at it.*

PILOT: *(V.O.)* Papa Victor Romeo this is Whiskey Tango Foxtrot ready for take-off over.

*SOUND CLIP: 'Reach for the Stars' by S Club 7 plays out through the bow.*

*Curtain.*

*FINAL CLIP 'POST SHOW FINALE' Images of CROOKSHANK and WINGWOMAN post RAF days are played out on the screen to original sounds bites from CROOKSHANK's BFBS radio shows and news interviews.*

WWW.OBERONBOOKS.COM

Follow us on www.twitter.com/@oberonbooks
& www.facebook.com/OberonBooksLondon